PreTime Piano

PRIMER LEVEL

Arranged by Nancy and Randall Faber

T0079436

This book belongs to: _____

Production Coordinator: Jon Ophoff
Editor: Isabel Otero Bowen
Design: Terpstra Design, San Francisco
Engraving: Dovetree Productions, Inc.

FABER
PIANO ADVENTURES®

HAL•LEONARD®

A NOTE TO TEACHERS

PreTime® Piano Disney offers an exciting set of contemporary and classic Disney favorites, arranged for the Primer student. The selections provide excellent practice of basic rhythms and beginning note reading. The pieces span primarily Bass C to Treble G.

Teacher duets provide vitality and color. They can be played and enjoyed with the teacher, a parent, sibling, or advancing student.

PreTime® Piano Disney designates the Primer Level of the PreTime to BigTime Piano Supplementary Library arranged by Faber & Faber. The series allows students to enjoy a favorite style at their current level of study. PreTime books are available in these styles: *Popular, Classics, Jazz & Blues, Rock'n Roll, Ragtime & Marches, Hymns, Kids' Songs, Christmas,* and the *Faber Studio Collection.*

Visit us at **PianoAdventures.com**.

Helpful Hints:

1. The student should know his/her part well before attempting ensemble playing. However, the duet part can be used first to demonstrate the rhythmic feel or "groove" of the song.

2. When performed up-to-tempo, some of the pieces have a feeling of cut time. An effective approach to these pieces is to have the student begin with the quarter note at a moderate tempo and then work up to a fast quarter-note beat. This essentially provides "built-in" slow practice, while also meeting the student's need for a sense of speed and mastery.

3. The selections appear in approximate order of difficulty.

4. The student may go through several *PreTime* books, at the teacher's discretion, before moving up to *PlayTime Piano* (Level 1).

THE PRETIME TO BIGTIME PIANO LIBRARY

PreTime® Piano   = Primer Level

PlayTime® Piano   = Level 1

ShowTime® Piano   = Level 2A

ChordTime® Piano = Level 2B

FunTime® Piano   = Level 3A–3B

BigTime® Piano   = Level 4 & above

ISBN 978-1-61677-697

Printed in U.S.A.

TABLE OF CONTENTS

*Based on the "Winnie the Pooh" works, by A. A. Milne and E. H. Shepard

Hand Position

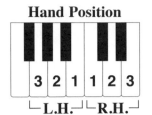

I Just Can't Wait to Be King

from *THE LION KING*

Music by ELTON JOHN
Lyrics by TIM RICE

Happily

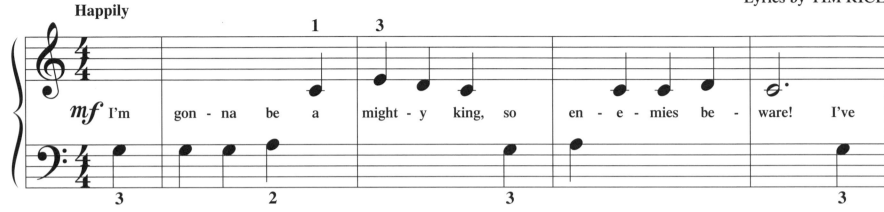

I'm gon - na be a might - y king, so en - e - mies be - ware! I've

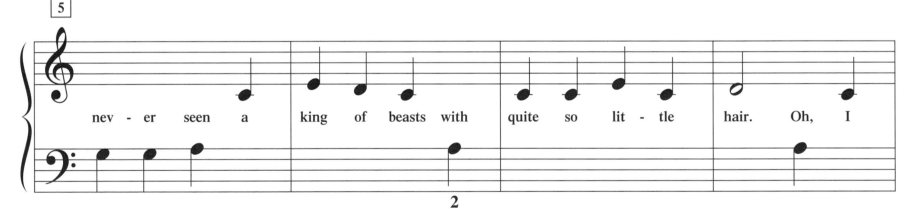

nev - er seen a king of beasts with quite so lit - tle hair. Oh, I

Teacher Duet: (Student plays 1 octave higher)

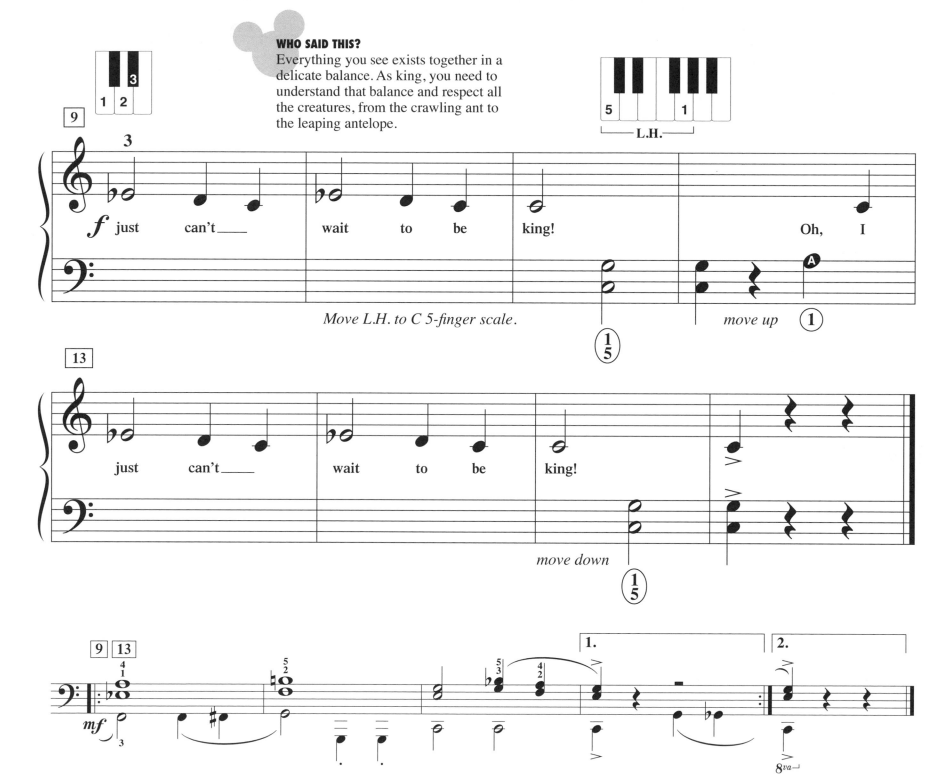

WHO SAID THIS?
Everything you see exists together in a delicate balance. As king, you need to understand that balance and respect all the creatures, from the crawling ant to the leaping antelope.

Move L.H. to C 5-finger scale.

move up

move down

ANSWER: Mufasa

It's a Small World

from Disney Parks' "it's a small world" Attraction

Words and Music by
RICHARD M. SHERMAN
and ROBERT B. SHERMAN

C 5-Finger Scale

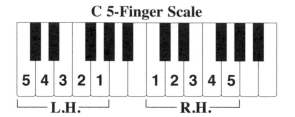

Playfully

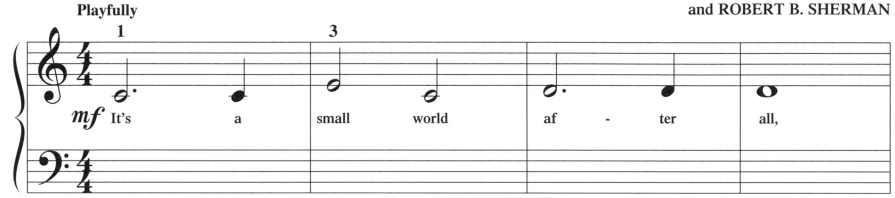

It's   a   small   world   af - ter   all,

Prepare the L.H. in the
C 5-finger scale.

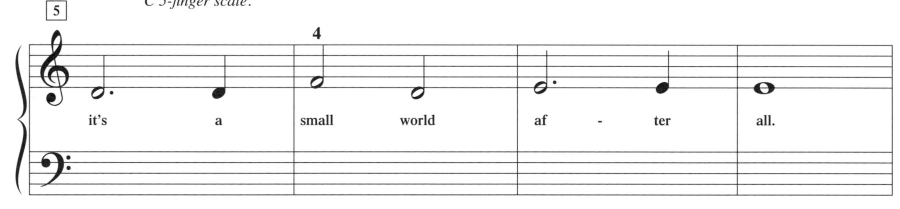

it's   a   small   world   af - ter   all.

Teacher Duet: (Student plays 1 octave higher)

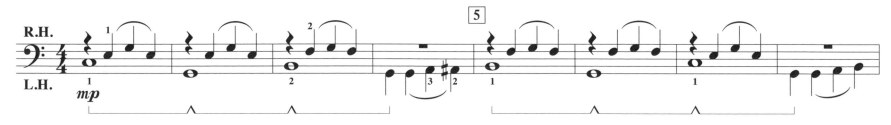

DID YOU KNOW?
The music for this Disney ride first used many national anthems all playing together—rather confusing! In the Sherman brothers' autobiography *Walt's Time,* the songwriters recalled, "Walt told us, 'I need something, and I need something right away. It should talk about unity and understanding and brotherly love, but don't get preachy. And I need it yesterday because it has to be translated into a whole lot of different languages.' We wrote the song so fast, we thought it was too simple to play for Walt…It seems to have turned out pretty well."

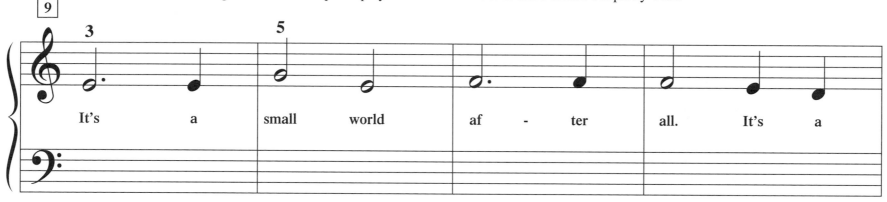

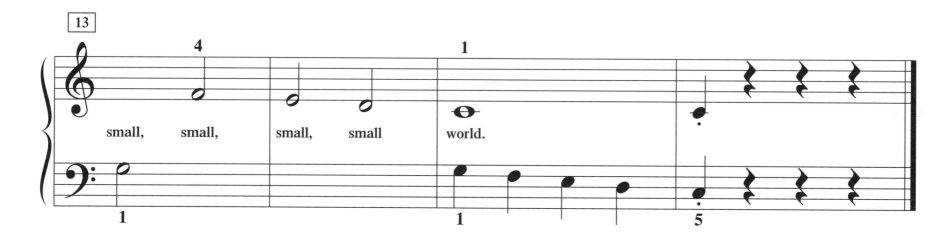

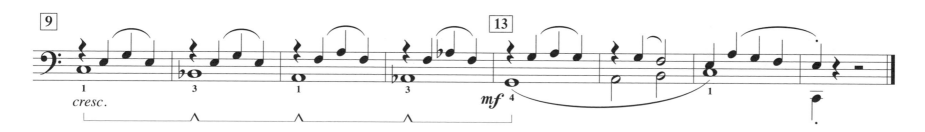

* For the duet the final low C for the student is optional.

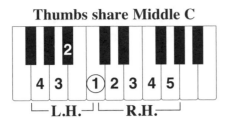

Supercalifragilisticexpialidocious

from *Mary Poppins*

Words and Music by
RICHARD M. SHERMAN
and ROBERT B. SHERMAN

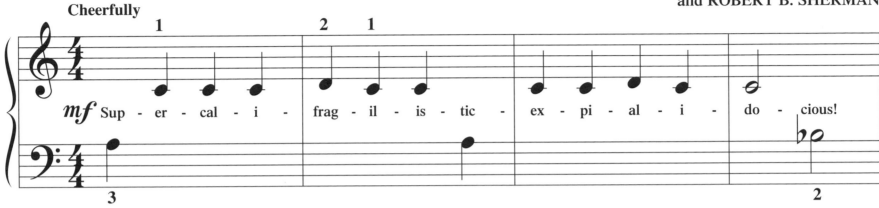

Sup - er - cal - i - frag - il - is - tic - ex - pi - al - i - do - cious!

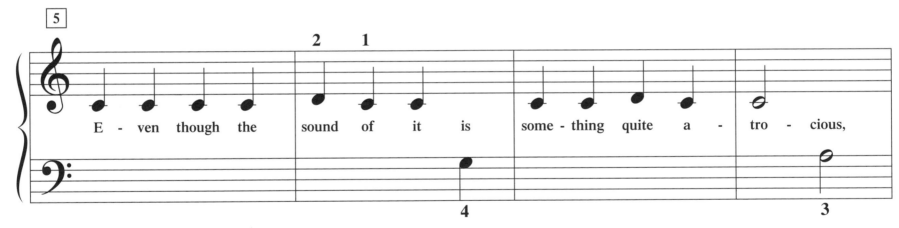

E - ven though the sound of it is some - thing quite a - tro - cious,

Teacher Duet: (Student plays 1 octave higher)

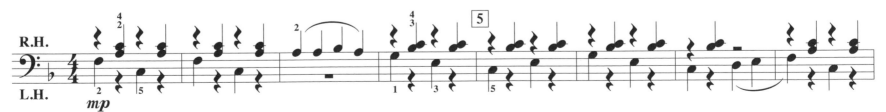

WHO SAID THIS?
You know, you can say it backwards,
which is Dociousaliexpiisticfragicalirupes —
but that's going a bit too far, don't you think?

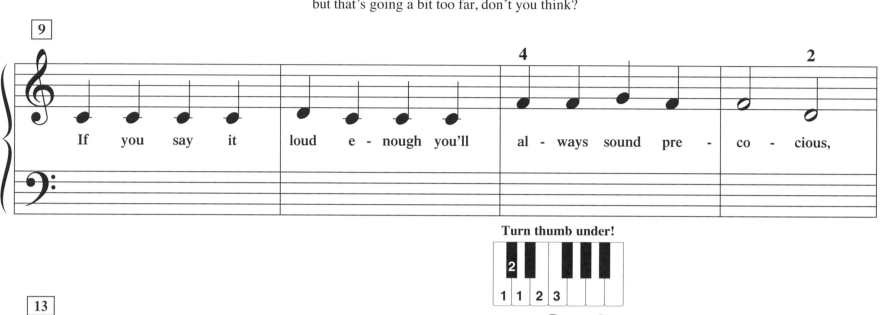

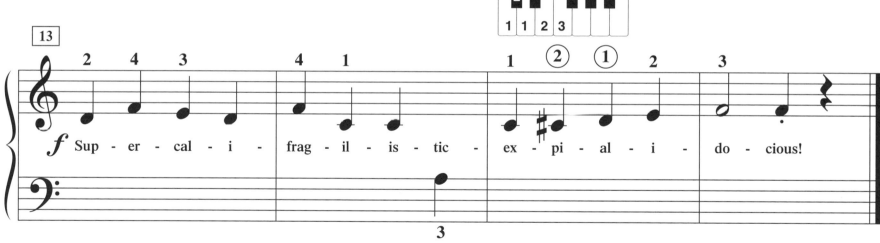

Winnie the Pooh*

from *THE MANY ADVENTURES OF WINNIE THE POOH*

Words and Music by
RICHARD M. SHERMAN
and ROBERT B. SHERMAN

Thumbs share Middle C

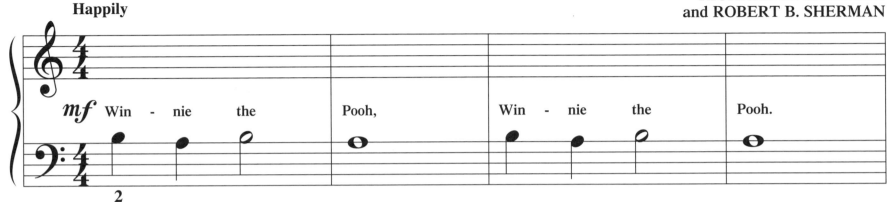

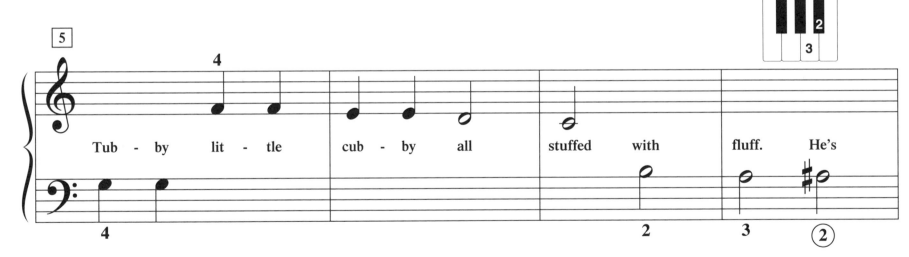

Teacher Duet: (Student plays 1 octave higher)

*Based on the "Winnie the Pooh" works,
by A. A. Milne and E. H. Shepard

Hop back to B!

9

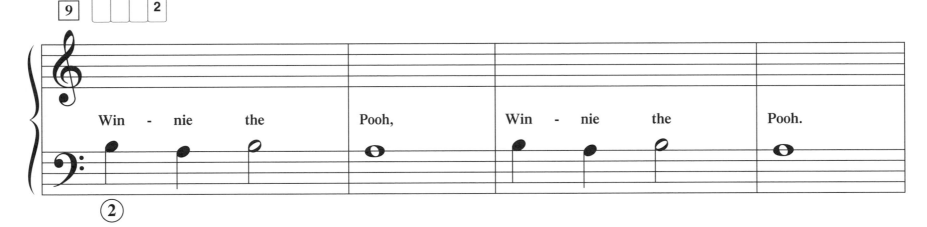

WHO SAID THIS?
And the only reason for being a bee…
is to make honey. And the only reason
for making honey is so I can eat it.

Win - nie the Pooh, Win - nie the Pooh.

13

L.H. ②*over*

Wil - ly nil - ly sil - ly 'ole bear. *f*

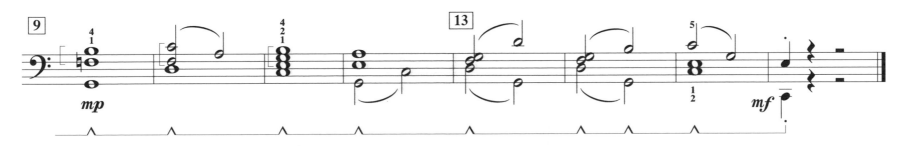

ANSWER: Winnie the Pooh

The Siamese Cat Song

from *LADY AND THE TRAMP*

Words and Music by
PEGGY LEE and
SONNY BURKE

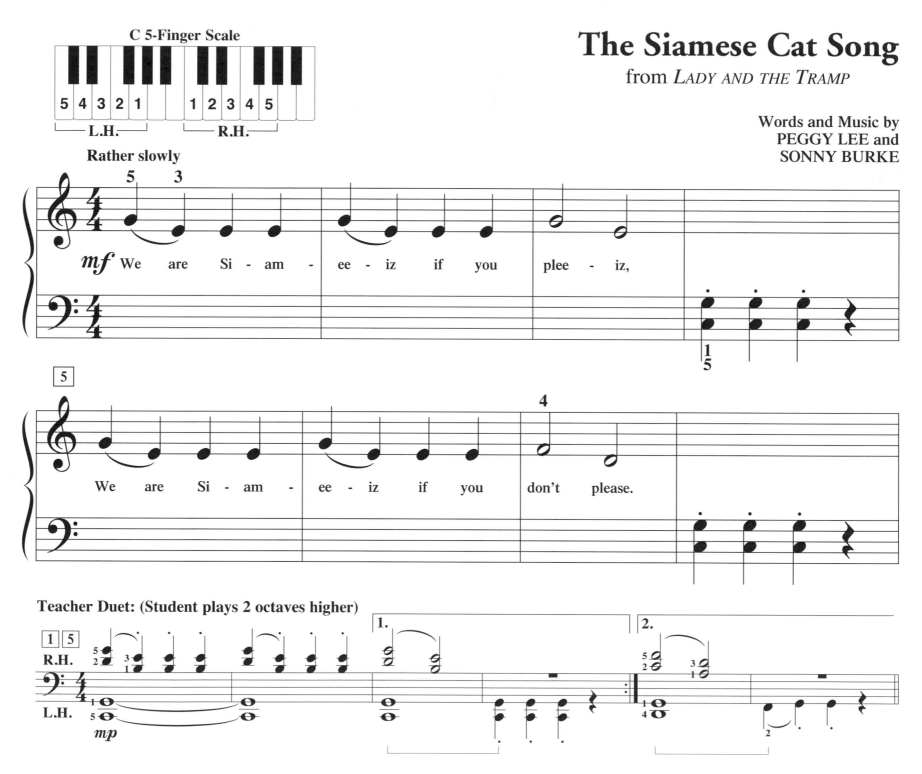

Teacher Duet: (Student plays 2 octaves higher)

WHO SAID THIS?

Okay, okay, okay! But remember this, Pigeon.
A human heart has only so much room for
love and affection. When a baby moves in,
the dog moves out.

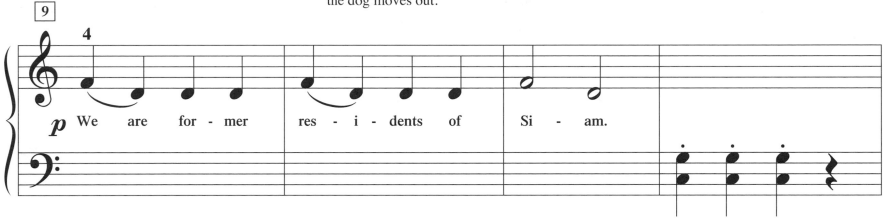

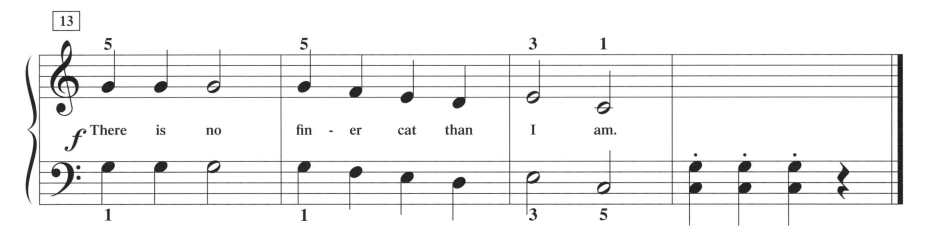

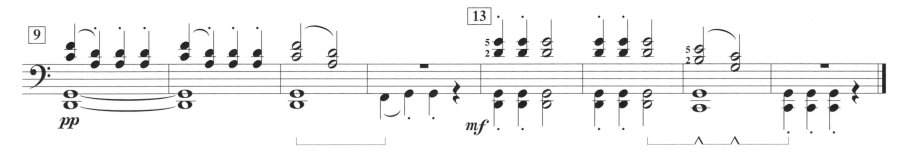

ANSWER: Tramp

I See the Light

From Walt Disney's *TANGLED*

WHO SAID THIS?
Woo-hoo! Best! Day! Ever!!

Music by ALAN MENKEN
Lyrics by GLENN SLATER

Teacher Duet: (Student plays 1 octave higher)

C 5-Finger Scale

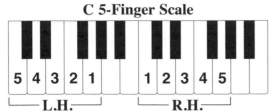

5 4 3 2 1 1 2 3 4 5
L.H.   R.H.

WHO SAID THIS?
Some people are
worth melting for.

Do You Want to
Build a Snowman?
from *FROZEN*

Music and Lyrics by
KRISTEN ANDERSON-LOPEZ
and ROBERT LOPEZ

Moderately

mf Do you want to build a snow - man?____

Come on, let's go and play! *(2 - 3 - 4)*

Teacher Duet: (Student plays 1 octave higher)

R.H.

L.H. mp

FF3039

Scales and Arpeggios

from *The Aristocats*

Words and Music by
RICHARD M. SHERMAN
and ROBERT B. SHERMAN

Hand Position

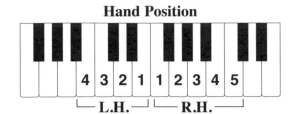

Cheerfully

mp Ev - 'ry tru - ly | cul - tured mu - sic | stu - dent | knows

Middle

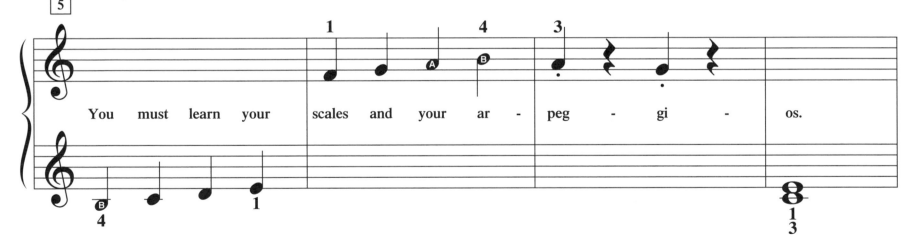

You must learn your | scales and your ar - | peg - gi - | os.

Teacher Duet: (Student plays 1 octave higher)

R.H. only

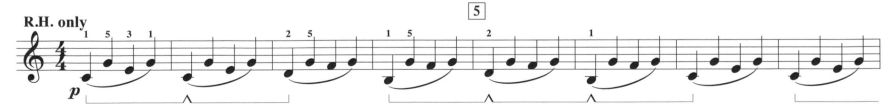

p

WHO SAID THIS?
Thank you, Miss Frou-Frou,
for letting me ride on your back.

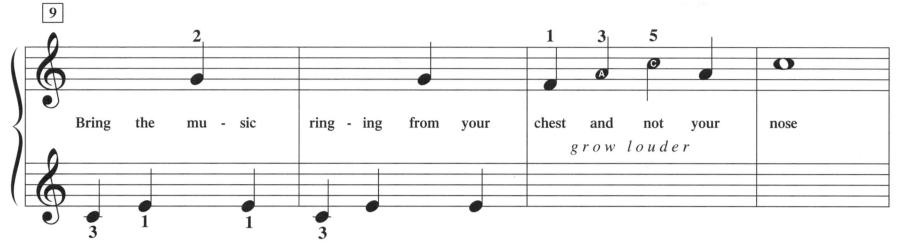

Bring the mu - sic ring - ing from your chest and not your nose

grow louder

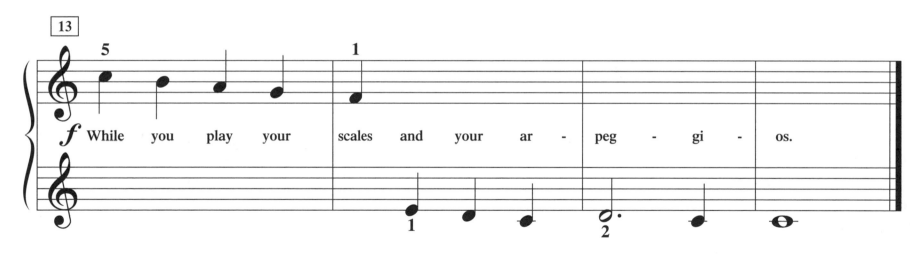

f While you play your scales and your ar - peg - gi - os.

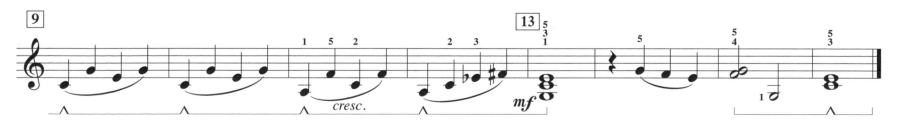

cresc. *mf*

Thumbs share Middle C

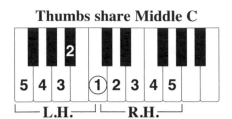

WHO SAID THIS?
You think. You wink. You do a double blink. You close your eyes and jump.

Step in Time
from *MARY POPPINS*

**Words and Music by
RICHARD M. SHERMAN
and ROBERT B. SHERMAN**

With spirit

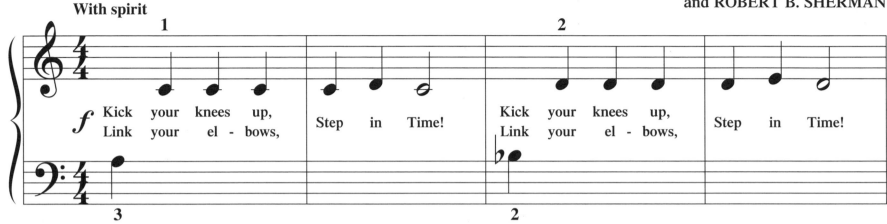

Kick your knees up,
Link your el - bows,   Step in Time!

Kick your knees up,
Link your el - bows,   Step in Time!

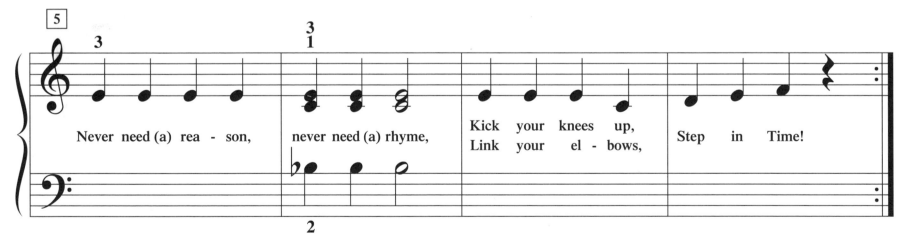

Never need (a) rea - son,   never need (a) rhyme,

Kick your knees up,
Link your el - bows,   Step in Time!

Teacher Duet: (Student plays 1 octave higher)

R.H.

L.H.   *mf*

ANSWER: Bret